1000

First Words
in French

How to use this book

Learning a new language is fun. The best way to learn French is to go to a country where it is spoken all around you. Talking with someone who knows the language very well is good, too. If possible, share this book with a grown–up who will help you to pronounce the words properly and ask you the questions under each picture.

You may notice some ways in which French is different from English. In English, there is only one word for **the**. We say **the house** and **the castle.** In French, there are two different words – **la maison** and **le chateau**. If you are talking about more than one thing, the word is **les**. Each time you learn a new word in French, try to learn the word for **the** that goes with it.

In the same way, **a house** and **a castle** are **une maison** and **un chateau**. **Some houses** and **some castles** are **des maisons** and **des chateaux**.

You may also notice that some French words have little signs above or below the letters. These help you to pronounce the word in the right way.

Have fun learning French!

1000

First Words in French

Written by Nicola Baxter

Translated by Guillame Dopffer

Illustrated by Susie Lacome

ARMADILLO

This edition is published by Armadillo, an imprint of Anness Publishing Ltd,
Blaby Road, Wigston, Leicestershire LE18 4SE; info@anness.com

www.annesspublishing.com

Anness Publishing has a new picture agency outlet for images for publishing, promotions
or advertising. Please visit our website www.practicalpictures.com for more information.

Produced for Anness Publishing Ltd by Nicola Baxter

Editorial consultant: Ronne Randall
Designer: Amanda Hawkes

PUBLISHER'S NOTE
Although the advice and information in this book are believed to be accurate and true at the time
of going to press, neither the authors nor the publisher can accept any legal responsibility or liability
for any errors or omissions that may have been made.

Manufacturer: Anness Publishing Ltd, Blaby Road, Wigston, Leicestershire LE18 4SE, England
For Product Tracking go to: www.annesspublishing.com/tracking
Batch: 5483-21720-1127

Sommaire

La Maison

une poubelle

un seau

une boite
à outils

une jardinière

un toît

une gouttière

un chemin

une cheminée

une échelle

une fenêtre

une porte

Who is in the garage?
Is the bucket blue?
Can you see two gloves?
Where are Teddy Bear's boots?

une radio   un pas   une bouteille   une collation   des   une tuile   une treille
de porte   thermos   briques

un projecteur

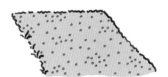

une allée

une sonnette

une serviette

une antenne

Qui est dans le garage?
Le seau est-il bleu?
Peux-tu trouver deux gants?
Où sont les bottes d'Ursule L'Ourson?

un gant

La Cuisine

un
bol-doseur

une
casserole

un livre
de cuisine

un grille-pain

un rouleau à
pâtisserie

un bocal

un réfrigérateur

une cuillère
en bois

une poêle

un torchon

un four à
micro-ondes

What is on the worktop?
Can you see the saucepan lid?
Who is looking in the refrigerator?
What could you use for mixing?

un plan de travail

 un tabouret

 une cuisinière

 une bouilloire

 un fer à repasser

 un évier

 un robot ménager

 du liquide vaisselle

 un tiroir

 un pense-bête

 un lave-vaisselle

 un égouttoir

 un bol-mixeur

Qu'y a-t-il sur le plan de travail?
Peux-tu trouver le couvercle de la casserole?
Qui fouille dans le réfrigérateur?
De quoi pourrais-tu te servir pour mélanger?

La Chambre à Coucher

une brosse à cheveux

une couette

un mobile   un peign

un lit

une penderie

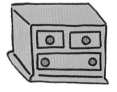

une commode

une table de chevet

un pyjama

une robe de chambre

un oreiller

What can you see in Teddy Bear's bedroom?
What is under the bedside table?
What color are Teddy Bear's pajamas?
What is on the bedside table?

des
pantoufles

des
chaussettes

un coffre

un poster

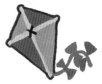
un
cerf-volant

un illustré

un abat-jour

une toise

une corbeille

un réveil

un dessin

un cintre

une tirelire

Que vois-tu dans la chambre d'Ursule L'Ourson?
Qu'y a-t-il sous la table de chevet?
De quelle couleur est le pyjama d'Ursule l'Ourson?
Qu'y a-t-il sur la table?

La Salle de Bains

 un savon

 une serviette

 une éponge

une brosse à dents

 une baignoire

 un lavabo

 du papier toilette

 une douche

un rideau de douche

 un tapis de bain

 une armoire à pharmacie

What color are the wall tiles?
What is on the bath mat?
How many toothbrushes can you see?
How many pawprints can you find?

 des toilettes

 un miroir

 une brosse à ongles

 un robinet

 une balance

 une serviette de bain

 du shampooing

 du bain-moussant

 un tube de dentifrice

 un jouet de bain

 des carreaux

 une brosse

 un canard

De quelle couleur sont les carreaux au mur?
Qu'y a-t-il sur le tapis de bain?
Combien de brosses à dents comptes-tu?
Combien de traces de pattes vois-tu?

Le Salon

un tapis

un fauteuil

une bibliothèque

un magazine

un aspirateur

une plante verte

un chiffon
à poussière

une
pendule

un rideau

un
lampadaire

un couss

What is on the sofa?
How many dusters can you see?
What is on the bookcase?
What color is the armchair?

 un journal

 un vase

 un magnétoscope

 une photo

 de la moquette

 un tableau

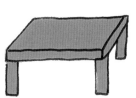 une table basse

 une télécommande

 un canapé

 une cheminée

 une télévision

 une chaîne hi-fi

 du papier peint

Qu'y a-t-il sur le canapé?
Combien de chiffons y a-t-il?
Qu'y a-t-il sur la bibliothèque?
De quelle couleur est le fauteuil?

15

Le Grenier

un berceau

une maison de poupée

une cage

une lucarne

une boite en carton

un cadre

une valise

un mannequin

des skis

une ampoule

une toile d'araignée

How many jars can you see?
What is on the sledge?
Can you see a bed?
What is red and white?

16

 de la
peinture

 un transat

 des
bouteilles

 un chapeau

 des pots
à confiture

 une trappe

 une canne à
pêche

 un fauteuil
à bascule

 des décorations
de Noël

 une machine
à coudre

 un cheval
à bascule

 des patins
à glace

Combien de pots à confiture vois-tu?
Qu'y a-t-il sur la luge?
Vois-tu un lit?
Qu'est-ce qui est rouge et blanc?

une luge

Le Jardin

une brouette

des cisailles

de la terre

une pelle

un pot

un arrosoir

un tuyau
d'arrosage

une fourche

du gazon

une tondeuse
à gazon

des
graines

What is on the grass?
What is in the wheelbarrow?
How many birds can you see?
What color is the watering can?

18

des feuilles

 un nichoir

une binette

 une fourche

une truelle

un perchoir

 une cabane

 une jardinière suspendue

 un râteau

 une haie

 des fleurs

 une fontaine

 un balai

Qu'y a-t-il sur l'herbe?
Qu'y a-t-il sur la brouette?
Combien d'oiseaux vois-tu ?
De quelle couleur est l'arrosoir?

La Rue

 une bicyclette

 un pigeon

 des bonbons

 un gâteau

 un trottoir

 une grille

 un lampadaire

 une poubelle

 un camion de livraison

 un chauffeur

 une poussette

How many wheels can you see?
Which store sells lollipops?
What color are the boots in the shoe store?
Do you like cakes?

 une école

 une pâtisserie

 un paquet

 une route

une sucette

 une bouche d'égout

une casque

 un sac à provisions

un magasin de chaussures

un panneau

 une confiserie

 une corde à sauter

 des bottes

Rue Lepic

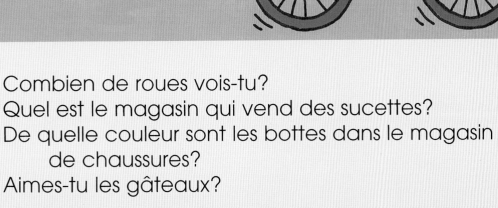

Combien de roues vois-tu?
Quel est le magasin qui vend des sucettes?
De quelle couleur sont les bottes dans le magasin
de chaussures?
Aimes-tu les gâteaux?

Le Supermarché

un porte-monnaie

de l'argent **des fruits**

un sac à main

des boites de conserve

un client

un caddie

une queue

un panier

un sac

une caisse-enregistreuse

How many bears are in the queue?
Can you see Teddy Bear?
Where is the milk?
What is on the conveyor belt?

22

du lait

 des clés

 un yaourt

 un carton

 du jus de fruits

du miel

 un code barre

 un vendeur

 un ticket de caisse

 un panneau

 un caissier

 des légumes

Combien d'ours y a-t-il dans la queue?
Peux-tu voir Ursule L'Ourson?
Où est le lait?
Qu'y a-t-il sur le tapis de la caisse?

 un tapis de caisse

L'École

une règle

un tableau noir

une carte
géographique

des crayons

de la pâte
à modeler

de la craie

des patères

une
maîtresse

des feutres

du papier

de l'eau

What is the teacher holding?
What do you need for painting?
How many pupils can you see?
What color is the ruler?

un élève

 un pinceau

 une gomme

 un portrait

 un aquarium

 un chevalet

 une boîte de couleurs

 l'alphabet

 un cahier

 un ordinateur

 un cartable

 un puzzle

 des ciseaux

Que tient la maîtresse?
De quoi as-tu besoin pour peindre?
Combien d'élèves vois-tu?
De quelle couleur est la règle?

Les Transports

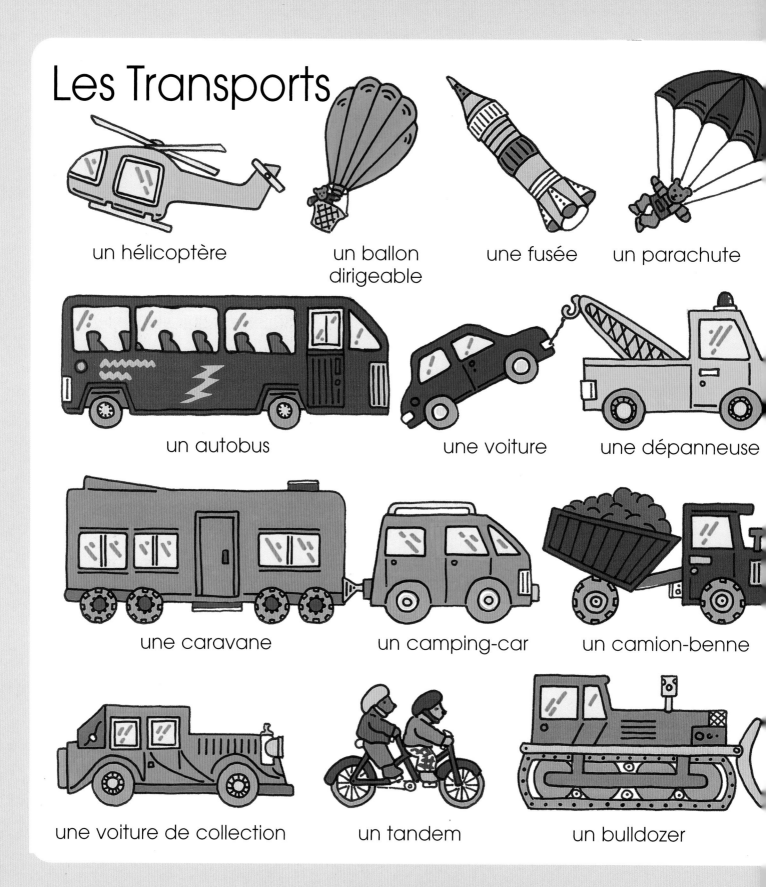

un hélicoptère

un ballon dirigeable

une fusée

un parachute

un autobus

une voiture

une dépanneuse

une caravane

un camping-car

un camion-benne

une voiture de collection

un tandem

un bulldozer

Can you see Teddy Bear?
What color is the refuse truck?
Which motorcar is very old?
How many motorcars can you see?

une voiture de course

un rouleau-compresseur

un camion à ordures

un poids-lourd

un kart

un camion

une motocyclette

un camion-citerne

une pelleteuse

un camion à plateau

un camion de déménagement

Où est Ursule L'Ourson?
De quelle couleur est le camion à ordures?
Quelle voiture est très vieille?
Combien de voitures vois-tu?

La Ferme

un mouton

un agneau

un cochon

un cochonne

des poussins

une poule

un chien

un cheval

un poulain

un fermier

une ferme

Where is the duck?
What is the farmer holding?
How many chicks does he have?
Is the tractor yellow?

28

 un canard

 un caneton

un chat

une souris

une barrière

une clotûre

un épouvantail

 une mare

 un coq

 une vache

 un veau

 un champ

 un tracteur

Où est le canard?
Que tient le fermier?
Combien de poussins a-t-il?
Est-ce que le tracteur est jaune?

Le Parc

un cornet
de glace

un toboggan

une balançoire

un coureur

un bac à sable

une fontaine

un parterre
de fleurs

un banc

des
genouillères

un oiseau

un klaxon

Is Teddy Bear on the swing?
What is in the hamper?
How many bears are wearing helmets?
How many wheels does a tricycle have?

 un tricycle

 une planche à roulettes

 une bascule

 des roues

 une malle

 un cerceau

 une balle

 un pique-nique

 un écureuil

 des sandwiches

 une trottinette

 des patins à roulettes

 un baladeur

Ursule L'Ourson est-il sur la balançoire?
Qu'y a-t-il dans la malle?
Combien d'ours portent des casques?
Combien y a-t-il de roues sur un tricycle?

Le Monde des Contes

une baguette magique

un puits magique

un champignon

un elfe

une fée

une lance

un bouclier

une couronne

une épée

un dragon

une armure

un chevalier

une princesse

Who can do magic?
What color is the dragon?
Where does a king live?
Who wears armor?

une bannière

un chapeau-claque

un page

une citrouille

un magicien

une cape

un prince une reine un roi

un géant un château

Qui peut faire de la magie?
De quelle couleur est le dragon?
Où vit un roi?
Qui porte une armure?

La Campagne

  une tente   un arbre   un randonneur   un pont

une forêt

une montagne

un champ

une rivière

un lac

une branche

un feu de camp

How many carriages does the engine have?
Who is sitting on a log?
Is the sleeping bag in the tent?
Is the rowing boat on the river?

un tronc

 une locomotive

 un wagon

 un buisson

 des jumelles

 une cascade

 une souche

 un village

 un rail de chemin de fer

 une barque

 une colline

 un sac de couchage

 des rochers

Combien de wagons sont derrière la locomotive?
Qui est assis sur une souche?
Le sac de couchage est-il dans la tente?
La barque est-elle sur la rivière?

Le Port

des
poissons

des
pagaies

une corde

une balise

des hublots

un sous-marin

un paquebot

un pêcheur

une grue

un chalutier

un bateau
à moteur

What can go under the water?
What are round windows on a boat called?
How many fish can you see?
What is on the jetty?

un gilet de
sauvetage

un crochet

une
ancre

un
homard

un mat

un kayak

du ski
nautique

un casier
à homard

une
combinaison

une jetée

un
porte-conteneurs

un plongeur

une bouée
de sauvetage

Qu'est-ce qui va sous l'eau?
Comment appelle-t-on les fenêtres rondes sur un bateau?
Combien de poissons vois-tu?
Qu'y a-t-il sur la jetée?

L'Aéroport

une cane

une boisson

un chariot
à bagages

un tableau
d'affichage

un bus

un avion

une tour
de contrôle

des toilettes

un
hangar

une
étiquette

un porte-
papiers

How many suitcases can you see?
Who is carrying a mop?
Can you see our Teddy Bear?
Have you ever flown in an airplane?

38

une valise

 un café

 une piste
d'atterissage

 un balai à
franges

 un agent
d'entretien

 des billets

 un appareil
photo

 une manche
à air

un pilote

 un comptoir
d'enregistrement

une hôtesse

 un sac à dos

 un téléphone

Combien de valises vois-tu?
Qui porte un balai à franges?
Vois-tu Ursule L'Ourson?
As-tu déjà pris l'avion?

L'Hôpital

 un plateau

 une infirmière

 de l'eau

 une bande

un drap

un médecin

une robe
de chambre

un
médicament

un visiteur

un
déambulateur

de la ouate

What is the nurse holding?
Who is in the elevator?
Is the doctor's coat red?
Have you ever been in hospital?

40

un
ascenseur

 un
infirmier

 une
montre

 une écharpe

 un
pansement

 une
seringue

une couverture

 une carte

 un plâtre

 une courbe de
température

 un
stéthoscope

 un
thermomètre

 un fauteuil
roulant

Que tient l'infirmière?
Qui est dans l'ascenseur?
La blouse du médecin est-elle rouge?
As-tu déjà été dans un hôpital?

41

À la Mer

un drapeau
de pirate

un
hippocampe

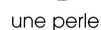
une chaîne

une perle

une baleine

un galion

un message dans
une bouteille

un requin

un nageur

un trésor

une méduse

What is on the island?
What is in the sea?
What goes in a keyhole?
Which is the biggest animal in the sea?

42

du corail

une pieuvre

un pirate

un dauphin

un pistolet

un bandeau

une huître

une carte

un trou de serrure

une île

une algue

une sirène

un palmier

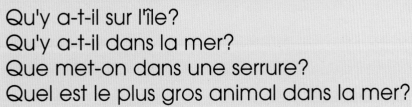

Qu'y a-t-il sur l'île?
Qu'y a-t-il dans la mer?
Que met-on dans une serrure?
Quel est le plus gros animal dans la mer?

Le Magasin de Jouets

une dinette

une boîte
à surprises

des crayons
de couleur

une toupie

une maison

un jeu de
société

une
marionnette

 un boulier

 des quilles

 un
chateau-fort

 une poupée

How many building bricks can you see?
Who is holding a glove puppet?
Which toys are for babies?
Which is your favorite toy?

 des perles
 un chariot
 un yoyo
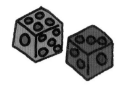 des dés
 des billes
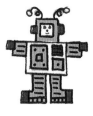 un robot
 des cônes

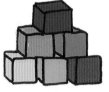 des briques

 une chenille

 des soldats

 un livre de coloriage

 une voiture à pédales

un costume de clown

Combien de briques vois-tu?
Qui tient une marionette?
Quels jouets sont pour les bébés?
Quel est ton jouet préféré?

L'Atelier

une clé   une   une tasse   une
       lampe-torche   perceuse

une poche

un calendrier

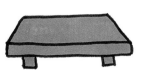

une étagère

une poignée
de porte

un mètre-
mesureur

des biscuits

l'arche de Noé

46

How many animals can you see?
What is on the workbench?
What is on the shelf?
What color is the door?

 une scie

 un tournevis

 des vis

 des clous

 un marteau

 des lunettes

 un canif

 du papier de verre

 un maillet

 une planche

 des animaux

 une pince

 un établi

Combien d'animaux vois-tu?
Qu'y a-t-il sur le plan de travail?
Qu'y a-t-il sur l'étagère?
De quelle couleur est la porte?

Le Bord de Mer

 un drapeau

 du sable

un coquillage

 la mer

 un château de sable

une étoile de mer

 un maillot de bain

un parasol

 des galets

 une épuisette

 des lunettes

How many legs does a starfish have?
How many sea shells can you see?
What is very cold?
What color is the flag?

48

 un crabe

 des palmes

 un voilier

 des brassards

 le soleil

 des vagues

 de la lotion solaire

 un phare

 une bouée

 un ballon de plage

 un caleçon de bain

 une mouette

 une glace à l'eau

Combien de branches une étoile de mer a-t-elle?
Combien de coquillages vois-tu?
Qu'est-ce qui est très froid?
De quelle couleur est le drapeau?

49

La Fête

un cadeau

un
clown

une bougie

un bouton

une paille

un chapeau

une part de
gâteau

une boisson
gazeuse

un gobelet

une nappe

un gâteau
d'anniversaire

How old is the birthday bear?
How old are you?
How many balloons can you see?
Who is under the table?

un gilet

 un ruban

 un ballon

 un nœud-papillon

 un masque

 un nœud

 colin-maillard

 du papier cadeau

 des cotillons

 une pochette-surprise

 une enveloppe

 une carte d'anniversaire

 une robe de fête

Quel âge a l'ours dont c'est l'anniversaire?
Quel âge as-tu?
Combien de ballons vois-tu?
Qui est sous la table?

Les Parties du Corps

le sourcil

les cheveux

le pouce

un doigt

la paume

la lèvre

la joue

le coude

le genou

le poignet

l'orteil

la main

la cheville

How many toes does Dolly have?
What color is her hair?
Do you have paws?
Are your eyes blue like Teddy's?

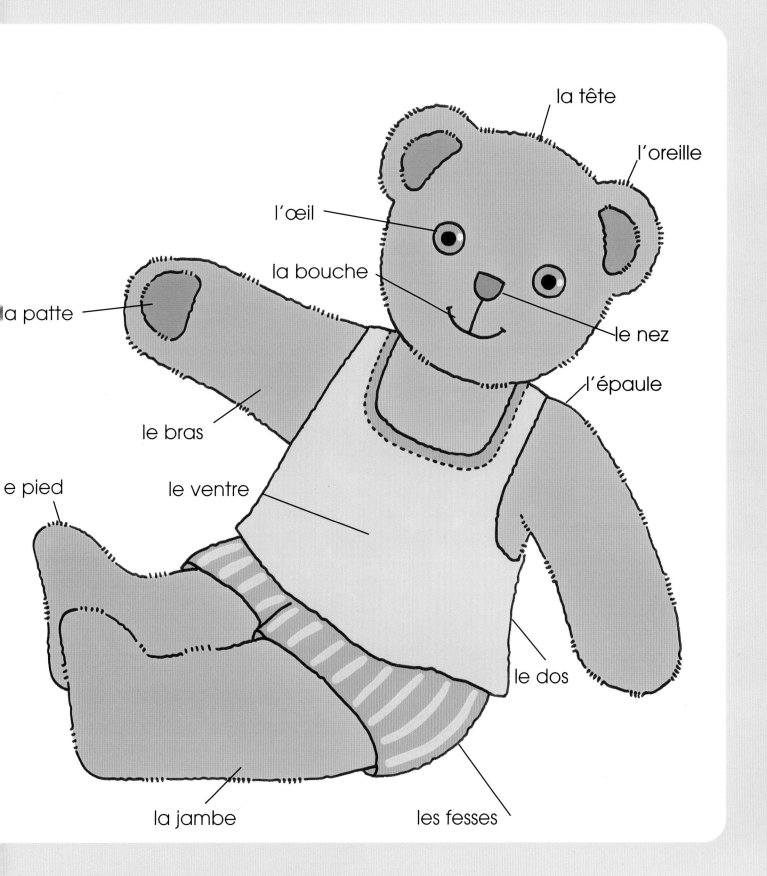

la tête

l'oreille

l'œil

la bouche

le nez

l'épaule

la patte

le bras

le pied

le ventre

le dos

la jambe

les fesses

Combien d'orteils a Dolly?
De quelle couleur sont ses cheveux?
As-tu des pattes?
Tes yeux sont-ils bleus comme ceux d'Ursule L'Ourson?

Des Ours Bien Occupés

ramper

être assis

lire

faire des câlins

chanter

boire

manger

écrire

saluer

se laver

se sécher

dormir

What do you like to do?
What is Teddy Bear doing?
What do babies like doing?
Are you sitting or standing?

shooter

sauter

faire du tricycle

bondir

marcher

s'habiller

courir

sauter à la corde

pousser

tirer

danser

être debout

Qu'aimes-tu faire?
Que fait Ursule L'Ourson?
Qu'aiment faire les bébés?
Es-tu assis ou debout?

Les Saisons

le printemps

l'été

l'automne

l'hiver

Which season is it now?
Is there snow in the summer?
When does Teddy Bear fly his kite?
What comes from clouds?

La Météo

le soleil　　la neige　　l'arc-en-ciel　　la glace　　une bourrasque

des stalactites　　le vent　　un flocon　　un nuage　　une tornade

un bonhomme
de neige　　la pluie　　la rosée　　la foudre　　la chaleur

l'innondation　　le givre　　le brouillard　　le froid　　des flaques

Quelle est la saison en ce moment?
Y a-t-il de la neige en été?
Quand Ursule L'Ourson fait-il voler son cerf-volant?
Qu'est ce qui vient des nuages?

Mes Aliments Préférés

du beurre

un biscuit

des céréales

du sucre

de la soupe

un hotdog

des frites

des sauces

du chocolat

du riz

des beignets

des spaghettis

What is your favorite food?
Do you like cheese?
How many spoons can you see?
What is on Teddy Bear's ears?

de la salade

un hamburger

une pizza

des haricots

un gâteau

du fromage

du pain

de la charcuterie

des fruits secs

de la farine

une omelette

une tarte

Quel est ton plat préféré?
Aimes-tu le fromage?
Combien de cuillères vois-tu?
Qu'y a-t-il sur les oreilles d'Ursule?

Les Sports et les Jeux

le cricket

le baseball

le rugby

le tennis

le saut en hauteur

le tir à l'arc

la course à deux

l'escalade

le plongeon

le saut à la perche

une équipe

la gymnastique

Can you see Teddy Bear?
Which sports need a ball?
Which is your favorite sport?
How many bears are waving?

le trampoline le vélo les haltères l'aviron

le patin à roulettes le golf le football la course en sac

le patin à glace le basketball les arts martiaux une coupe

Vois-tu Teddy L'ourson ?
Combien de ballons vois-tu ?
Quel est ton sport préféré ?
Combien d'oursons sont en train de saluer?

Un Peu de Musique!

un tambourin

un triangle

des cymbales

des maracas

un violon

un synthétiseur

un trombone

un pipeau

un pupître

des notes

un chef d'orchestre

un violoncelle

Can you play these instruments?
Which instruments do you blow?
Which instruments have strings?
Which instruments do you hit?

une flûte

une partition

un hautbois

une trompette

un saxophone

un banjo

un xylophone

une guitare

une harpe

un piano

des timbales

Sais-tu jouer de ces instruments?
Dans quels instruments souffle-t-on?
Quels sont les instruments qui ont des cordes?
Sur quels instruments peut-on frapper?

Les Bébés Ours

 un hochet un bavoir un biberon

 une tétine

des botons

une alarme

un matelas
à langer

un livre
de bébé

une tirelire

une
grenouillère

un berceau

Do baby bears sleep in a big bed?
What color is the trainer cup?
What are the baby bears wearing?
Do you have a moneybox?

une
poussette

un
châle

une
couche

des lingettes

un anneau
de dentition

lun pot

une chaise
haute

une timbale

un livre en tissu

un livre cartonné

une peluche

un matelas

un sac à langer

Les petits oursons dorment-ils dans des grands lits?
De quelle couleur est la tasse de bébé?
Que portent les bébés?
As-tu une tirelire?

Les Nombres

une maison

deux voitures

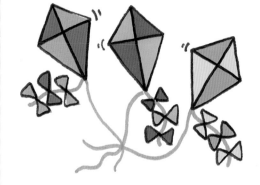

trois cerf-volants

quatre lapins

cinq ballons

six canards

sept fraises

huit crayons

neuf fleurs

dix coeurs

What color are the rabbits?
How many bears can you see?
How many flowers can you count?
What is five plus seven?

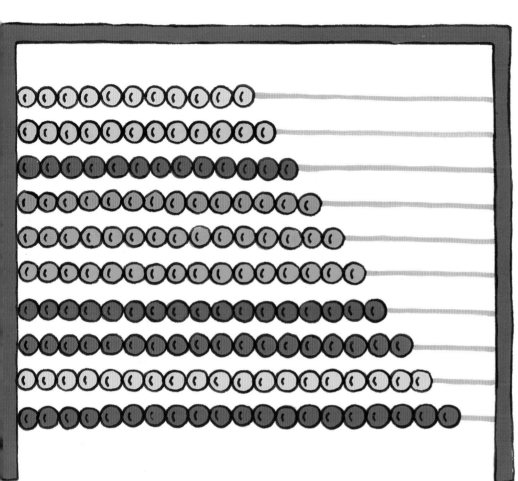

11 onze

12 douze

13 treize

14 quatorze

15 quinze

16 seize

17 dix-sept

18 dix-huit

19 dix-neuf

20 vingt

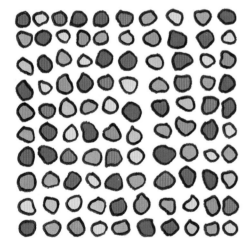

100 cent

troisième   second   premier

De quelle couleur sont les lapins?
Combien d'ours vois-tu?
Combien de fleurs comptes-tu?
Combien font cinq plus sept?

Les Couleurs

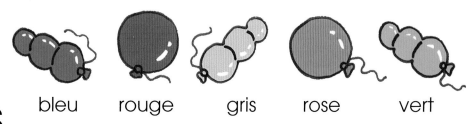

bleu   rouge   gris   rose   vert

blanc

noir

jaune

marron

violet

orange

bleu marine

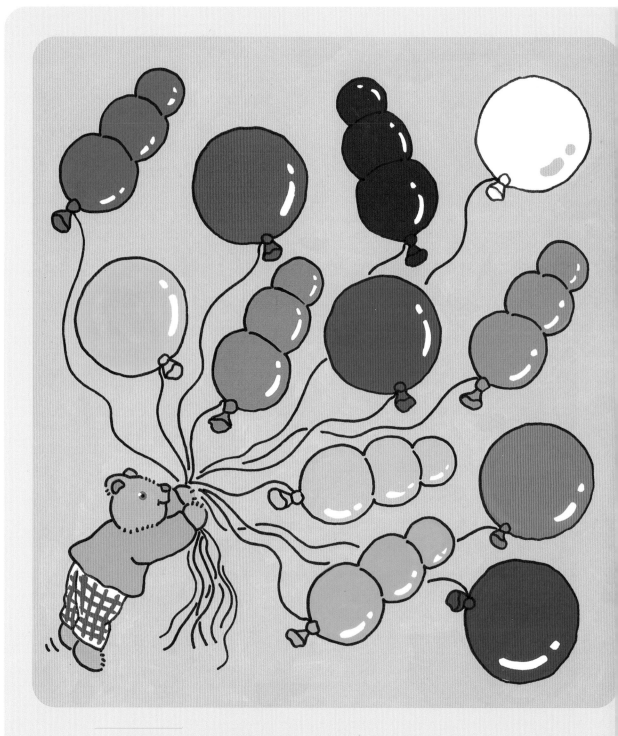

What is your favorite color?
What color is Teddy Bear's top?
Are there zigzags on Teddy Bear's pants?
Which shape is pink?

Les Formes

 un cœur

 des rayures

 un cercle

 un carré

 une étoile

 un losange

 un rectangle

 des zigzags

 des pois

 un ovale

 un triangle

un damier

Quelle est ta couleur préférée?
De quelle couleur est le tricot d'Ursule?
Il y a-t-il des zigzags sur le pantalon d'Ursule?
Quelle forme est rose?

69

Les Vêtements

un bonnet

un mouchoir

des moufles

des chaussures de sport

une écharpe

un jean

une veste

un chemisier

un débardeur

un pantalon

un pullover

What do you wear on a hot day?
What do you wear on a cold day?
What color are the mittens?
What are you wearing now?

70

 un anorak

 des bottes

 un short

une jupe

une culotte

 un tee-shirt

 une pince à linge

 des chaussures

 une salopette

 une chemise

 un manteau

une cravate

 des collants

Que portes-tu quand il fait chaud?
Que portes-tu quand il fait froid?
De quelle couleur sont les moufles?
Que portes-tu aujourd'hui?

La Famille

une arrière grand-mère   un arrière grand-père

une grand-mère   un grand-père   une grand-tante   un grand-oncle

un père   une mère   une tante   un oncle

une sœur   Ursule L'Ourson   un frère   une cousine   des jumeaux

Do you have any brothers or sisters?
How many brothers does Teddy Bear have?
How are you feeling now?
Are you frightened of spiders?

Les Émotions

avoir peur

être heureux

être timide

avoir honte

s'ennuyer

être fâché

être pensif

être triste

être fier

être désolé

As-tu des frères et sœurs?
Combien de frères a Ursule?
Comment te sens-tu aujourd'hui?
As-tu peur des araignées?

Les Fruits

une poire

une banane

de la pastèque

une lime

une framboise

des grains de raisin

des myrtilles

une figue

une mangue

de la rhubarbe

une groseille

Which is your favorite fruit?
How many bananas can you see?
What is Teddy Bear holding?
Which fruits are red?

74

une
orange

 une pêche

 un
citron

 une prune

 un
abricot

 une cerise

une
pomme

 une papaye

 un
pamplemousse

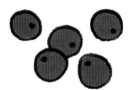 une fraise

 des airelles

 une clémentine

 un ananas

Quel est ton fruit préféré?
Combien de bananes vois-tu?
Que tient Ursule L'Ourson?
Quels fruits sont rouges?

Les Légumes

des champignons

une carotte

des broccolis

un poivron rouge

des petits pois

un poireau

un épi de maïs

un oignon

une pomme
de terre

un chou-fleur

des tomates

du céleri

Do you like carrots?
What is Teddy Bear eating?
Which vegetables are green?
What is your favorite vegetable?

une laitue

une betterave

des flageolets

un panais

un concombre

des radis

une patate douce

des haricots verts

un navet

des herbes

un chou

une courgette

Aimes-tu les carrottes?
Que mange Ursule L'Ourson?
Quels légumes sont verts?
Quel est ton légume préféré?

Les Fleurs

un
coquelicot

un iris

une
marguerite

une
campanule

une pensée

une jonquille

un dahlia

un tournesol

un œillet

un lys

une rose

Which flowers are yellow?
Which flower grows very tall?
What is under the cup?
What is Teddy Bear holding?

78

À Table!

 une petite cuillère

 du poivre

 du sel

 une soucoupe

une tasse

 une assiette

 un couteau

 une fourchette

 une cuillère

 un set de table

 un verre

 une carafe d'eau

Quelles fleurs sont jaunes?
Quel est la fleur qui pousse le plus haute?
Qu'y a-t-il sous la tasse?
Que tient Ursule L'Ourson?

Les Contraires

lent   rapide   grand   petit

grand   petit   ouvert   fermé

allumé   éteint   au pied   au sommet

Is an elephant small?
Is this book open or shut?
Are you inside or outside?
Are balloons heavy?

en haut

en bas

usé

neuf

plein

vide

léger

lourd

dedans

dehors

mince

gros

Les éléphants sont-ils petits?
Ce livre est-il ouvert ou fermé?
Es-tu à l'intérieur où à l'extérieur?
Les ballons sont-ils lourds?

Les Oiseaux

des œufs

un bec

une c...

une plume

un nid

un hibou

un macareux

un toucan

un pingouir

un paon

une autruche

un émeu

What is in the nest?
How many beaks can you see?
Which birds are black and white?
Which birds are eating fishes?

un martin-
pêcheur

une hirondelle

un kiwi

un colibri

un albatros

un vautour

une oie

une dinde

un flamand
rose

un pélican

une cigogne

un cygne

Qu'y a-t-il dans le nid?
Combien de becs vois-tu?
Quels oiseaux sont noir et blanc?
Quels oiseaux sont en train de manger des poissons?

Les Petites Bêtes

une abeille

un escargot

une coccinelle

un lézard

un ver

un papillon

une guêpe

une chenille

un scarabée

un mille-pattes

un caméléon

Which minibeasts have wings?
Which minibeast has six black spots?
Which minibeast carries its own house?
Which minibeasts do not have legs?

un papillon de nuit   une fourmi   une sauterelle   une limace   une mouche   une puce   une chrysalide

une mante religieuse

une tarantule

une grenouille

un scolopendre

une libellule

une araignée

Quels insectes ont des ailes ?
Quel est l'insecte qui a six points noirs?
Quel est la petite bête qui porte sa maison sur son dos?
Quelles sont les petites bêtes qui n'ont pas de pattes?

Les Animaux Sauvages

un koala

un rhinocéros

un tatou

un kangourou

un ours blanc

un gorille

une girafe

un singe

un tigre

un éléphant

un serpent

un panda

Which animal is very tall?
Which animal is very big?
Which animal is Teddy Bear feeding?
Which is your favorite animal?

un raton-laveur   un bison   un porc-épic   un zèbre

un ours   un crocodile   un chameau   un lion

un loup   un léopard   un castor   un hippopotame

Quel animal est très grand?
Quel animal est très gros?
Quel animal Ursule L'Ourson est-il en train de nourrir?
Quel est ton animal préféré?

Les Animaux Domestiques

une niche   un chaton   un hamster   un clapier

un canari

un lapin

un perroquet

une perruche

un cochon d'Inde

de la nourriture pour poisson

un poisson rouge

Do you have a pet?
Who lives in a kennel?
Where is the rabbit?
What is in the fish tank?

 un chiot

 des bulles

 une brosse

 une tortue

 un os

 une laisse

 un collier

 une écuelle pour chien

 un panier à chat

 un aquarium

 une trappe

 une tortue marine

 de l'eau

As-tu un animal domestique?
Qui vit dans une niche?
Où est le lapin?
Qu'y a-t-il dans l'aquarium?

Les Mots

a

abacus **un boulier**
airplane **un avion**
alarm clock **un réveil**
albatross **un albatros**
alphabet **l'alphabet**
anchor **une ancre**
angry **être fâché**
animals **des animaux**
ankle **la cheville**
anorak **un anorak**
ant **une fourmi**
antenna **une antenne**
apple **une pomme**
apricot **un abricot**
aquarium **un aquarium**
archery **le tir à l'arc**
arm **le bras**
armadillo **un tatou**
armbands **de brassards**
armchair **un fauteuil**
armor **une armure**
ashamed **avoir honte**
aunt **une tante**

b

baby alarm **une alarme**
baby record book **un
livre de bébé**
back **le dos**
baggage trolley **un
chariot à bagages**
ball **une balle**
balloon **un ballon**
banana **une banane**
bandage **une bande**
banjo **un banjo**
banner **une bannière**
barcode **un code barre**
baseball **le baseball**
basketball **le basketball**
bathrobe **une robe
de chambre**
bathroom cabinet
**une armoire
à pharmacie**

bathroom scales **une
balance**
bathtub **une baignoire**
bath mat **un tapis
de bain**
bath towel **une
serviette de bain**
bath toy **un jouet
de bain**
beachball **un ballon
de plage**
beads **des perles**
beak **un bec**
beans **des haricots**
bear **un ours**
beaver **un castor**
bed **un lit**
bedside table **une
table de chevet**
bedspread **une couette**
bee **une abeille**
beet **une betterave**
beetle **un scarabée**
bench **un banc**
bib **un bavoir**
bicycle **une bicyclette**
big **grand**
binoculars **des jumelles**
bird **un oiseau**
bird table **un perchoir**
birthday cake **un
gâteau d'anniversaire**
birthday card **une
carte d'anniversaire**
black **noir**
blanket **une couverture**
blindman's buff
colin-maillard
blouse **un chemisier**
blue **bleu**
bluebell **une campanule**
blueberries **de myrtilles**
board book **un livre
cartonné**
board game **un jeu
de société**

bone **un os**
bookcase **une
bibliothèque**
bootees **des botons**
boots **des bottes**
bored (to be) **s'ennuyer**
bottles **des bouteilles**
bottom (position) **sedere**
bow **un noeud**
bow tie **un noeud-
papillon**
branch **une branche**
bread **du pain**
bricks **des briques**
bridge **un pont**
broad beans **des
flageolets**
broccoli **des broccolis**
broom **un balai**
brother **un frère**
brown **marron**
brush **une brosse**
bubble bath **du bain-
moussant**
bubbles **des bulles**
bucket **un seau**
budgerigar **une
perruche**
buffalo **un bison**
buggy **une poussette**
building blocks **des
briques**
bulldozer **un bulldozer**
buoy **une balise**
bureau **une commode**
bus **un autobus**
bush **un buisson**
butter **du beurre**
butterfly **un papillon**
buttocks **les fesses**
button **un bouton**

c

cabbage **un chou**
cage **une cage**
cake **un gâteau**

cake store **un
pâtisserie**
calendar **un calendrier**
calf **un veau**
camel **un chameau**
camera **un appareil
photo**
camp fire **un feu de
camp**
camper van **un
camping-car**
canary **un canari**
candies **des bonbons**
candle **une bougie**
canoe **un kayak**
cans **des boîtes
de conserve**
car transporter **un
camion à plateau**
card **une carte**
cardboard box **une boîtes
en carton**
carnation **un œillet**
carpet **de la moquette**
carriage **un wagon**
carrier bag **un sac**
carton **un carton**
cashier **un caissier**
castle **un château**
cat **un chat**
cat basket **un panier
à chat**
cat flap **une trappe**
caterpillar **une chenille**
cauliflower **un chou-fleur**
celery **du céleri**
cello **un violoncelle**
centipede **un
scolopendre**
cereal **des céréales**
chain **une châine**
chalk **de la craie**
chalkboard **un
tableau noir**
chameleon **un caméléon**
changing bag **un sac**

à langer

changing mat **un matelas à langer**

check-in desk **un comptoir d'enregistrement**

checks **un damier**

cheek **la joue**

cheese **du fromage**

cherry **une cerise**

chest (box) **une coffre**

chicks **des poussins**

chimney **une cheminée**

chocolate **du chocolat**

Christmas decorations **des décorations de Noël**

chrysalis **une chrysalide**

circle **un cercle**

cleaner **un agent d'entretien**

climbing **l'escalade**

clipboard **un porte-papiers**

cloak **un cape**

clock **une pendule**

closet **une penderie**

cloth book **un livre en tissu**

clothes pin **un pince à linge**

cloud **un nuage**

clown **un clown**

clown outfit **un costume de clown**

coat **un manteau**

coat hooks **des patères**

coathanger **un cintre**

cockerel **un coq**

coffee **un café**

coffee table **un table basse**

cold **le froid**

collar **un collier**

colored pencils **des crayons de couleur**

coloring book **un livre de coloriage**

comb **un peigne**

comic **un illustré**

computer **un ordinateur**

conductor **un chef d'orchestre**

container ship **un porte-conteneurs**

control tower **une tour de contrôle**

conveyor belt **un tapis de caisse**

cookbook **un livre de cuisine**

cookies **des biscuits**

coral **du corail**

cot **un berceau**

cotton wool **de la ouate**

cousin **une cousine (un cousin)**

cow **une vache**

crab **un crabe**

cradle **un berceau**

cranberries **des airelles**

crane **une grue**

crawling **ramper**

crayons **des crayons**

cricket **le cricket**

crocodile **un crocodile**

crown **une couronne**

cucumber **un concombre**

cuddling **faire des câlins**

cuddly toy **une peluche**

cup **une tasse**

cycling **le vélo**

cymbals **des cymbales**

d

daffodil **une jonquille**

dahlia **un dahlia**

daisy **une marguerite**

dancing **danser**

deck chair **un transat**

delivery van **un camion de livraison**

dew **la rosée**

diamond **un losange**

diaper **une couche**

dice **des dés**

digger **une pelleteuse**

dish towel **un torchon**

dishwasher **un lave-vaisselle**

dishwashing liquid **du liquide vaisselle**

diver **un plongeur**

diving **le plongeon**

doctor **un médecin**

dog **un chien**

dog bowl **une écuelle pour chien**

doll **une poupée**

doll's house **une maison de poupée**

dolphin **un dauphin**

door **une porte**

doorbell **une sonnette**

doorknob **une poignée de porte**

doorstep **un pas de porte**

doughnuts **des beignets**

down **en bas**

dragon **un dragon**

dragonfly **une libellule**

drain **une bouche d'égout**

draining board **un égouttoir**

drape **un rideau**

drawer **un tiroir**

drawing **un dessin**

dressing **s'habiller**

dressmaker's dummy **un mannequin**

drill **une perceuse**

drink **une boisson**

drinking **boire**

drinking straw **une paille**

driver **un chauffeur**

driveway **une allée**

drying **se sécher**

duck **un canard**

duckling **un caneton**

dumper truck **un camion-benne**

dungarees **une salopette**

duster **un chiffon à poussière**

e

ear **l'oreille**

easel **un chevalet**

eating **manger**

egg **un œuf**

eight **huit**

eighteen **dix-huit**

elbow **le coude**

elephant **un éléphant**

elevator **un ascenseur**

eleven **onze**

elf **un elfe**

empty **vide**

emu **un émeu**

engine **une locomotive**

envelope **une enveloppe**

eraser **une gomme**

evergreen plant **une plante verte**

exercise book **un cahier**

eye **l'oeil**

eye patch **un bandeau**

eyebrow **le sourcil**

f

fairy **une fée**

fall **l'automne**

farmer **un fermier**

farmhouse **une ferme**

fast **rapide**

fat **gros**

father **un père**

faucet **un robinet**

feather **une plume**

feeer cup **une timbale**

feeding bottle **un biberon**

felt pens **des feutres**

fence **une clôture**

field **un champ**

fifteen **quinze**

fig **une figue**

fingers **un doigt**

fireplace **une cheminée**

first **premier**

fish **un poisson**

fish food **de la nourriture pour poisson**

fish tank **un aquarium**

fisherman **un pêcheur**

fishing boat **un chalutier**

fishing net **une épuisette**

fishing rod **une canne à pêche**

five **cinq**

flag **un drapeau**

flamingo **un flamand rose**

flashlight **une lampe-torche**

flask **une bouteille thermos**

flea **une puce**

flippers **des palmes**

flood **l'innondation**

flour **de la farine**

flower bed **un parterre de fleurs**

flowerpot **un pot**

flowers **des fleurs**

flute **une flûte**

fly **une mouche**

foal **un poulain**

fog **le brouillard**

food mixer **un robot ménager**

foot **le pied**

forest **une forêt**

fork (garden) **une fourche**

fork (table) **une fourchette**

fort **un château-fort**

fountain **une fontaine**

four **quatre**

fourteen **quatorze**

fries **des frites**

frightened **avoir peur**

frog **une grenouille**

frost **le givre**

fruit **des fruits**

frying pan **une poêle**

full **plein**

g

gale **une bourrasque**

galleon **un galion**

gate **une barrière**

giant **un géante**

giraffe **un girafe**

glass **un verre**

glove **un gant**

glove puppet **une marionette**

goggles **des lunettes**

go-kart **un kart**

goldfish **un poisson rouge**

golf **le golf**

goose **une oie**

gooseberry **une groseille**

gorilla **un gorille**

grandfather **un grand-père**

grandmother **une grand-mère**

grapefruit **un pamplemousse**

grapes **des grains de raisin**

grasshopper **une sauterelle**

gray **gris**

great aunt **une grand-tante**

great grandfather **un arrière grand-père**

great grandmother **une arrière grand-mère**

great uncle **un grand-oncle**

green **vert**

green beans **des haricots verts**

guinea pig **un cochon d'Inde**

guitar **une guitare**

gull **une mouette**

gymnastics **le gymnastique**

h

hair **les cheveux**

hairbrush **une brosse peigne**

hamburger **un hamburger**

hammer **un marteau**

hamper **une malle**

hamster **un hamster**

hand **la main**

hand fork **une fourche**

handbag **un sac à main**

handkerchief **un mouchoir**

hangar **un hangar**

hanging basket **une jardinière suspendue**

happy **être heureux**

harp **une harpe**

hat **un chapeau**

head **une tête**

heart **un cœur**

heat **la chaleur**

heavy **lourd**

hedge **une haie**

height chart **une toise**

helicopter **un hélicoptère**

hen **une poule**

herbs **des herbes**

hi-fi **une chaîne hi-fi**

high chair **une chaise haute**

high jump **le saut en hauter**

hill **un colline**

hippopotamus **un hippopotame**

hoe **une binette**

honey **du miel**

hook **un crochet**

hoop **un cerceau**

hooter **un klaxon**

horse **un cheval**

hose **un tuyua d'arrosage**

hot-air-balloon **un un ballon dirigeable**

hotdog **un hotdog**

house **une maison**

hummingbird **un colibri**

hundred **cent**

hutch **un clapier**

i

ice **la glace**

ice cream **un cornet de glace**

ice skates **de patins à glace**

ice skating **le patin à glace**

iced lolly **une glace à l'eau**

icicles **des stalactites**

information board **un tableau d'affichage**

inside **dedans**

iris **un iris**

iron **un fer à repasser**

island **une île**

j

jacket **une veste**

Jack-in-the-box **une boîte à surprises**

jars **des pots à confiture**

jeans **un jean**

jellyfish **une méduse**

jetty **une jetée**

jogger **un coureur**

judo **le judo**

juggernaut **un poids-lourd**

juice **du jus de fruits**

jumping **sauter**

k

kangaroo **un kangourou**

kennel **une niche**

kettle **une bouilloire**

keyboard **un synthétiseur**

keyhole **un trou de serrure**

keys **des clés**

kicking (a football) **shooter**

king **un roi**

kingfisher **un martin-pêcheur**

kite **un cerf-volant**

kitten **un chaton**

kiwi **un kiwi**

knee **le genou**

knee pads **des genouillères**

knife **un couteau**

knight **un chevalier**

koala **un koala**

l

label **une étiquette**

ladder **un échelle**

ladybird **une coccinelle**

lake **un lac**

lamb **un agneau**

lamp **un lampadaire**

lance **une lance**

lawnmower **une tondeuse à gazon**

lead (dog's) **un laisse**

leaping **bondir**

leaves **des feuilles**

leek **un poireau**

leg **la jambe**

lemon **un citron**

leopard **un léopard**

lettuce **une laitue**

life buoy **une bouée de sauvetage**

life vest **un gilet de sauvetage**

light (weight) **léger**

light bulb **une ampoule**

lighthouse **un phare**

lightning **la foudre**

lily **un lys**

lime **une lime**

liner **un paquebot**

lion **un lion**

lip **la lèvre**

little **petit**

lizard **un lézard**

lobster **un homard**

lobster pot **un caisier à homard**

log **une souche**

lollipop **une sucette**

m

magazine **un magazine**

magician **un magicien**

mallet **un maillet**

mango **une mangue**

map **une cart géographique**

maracas **des maracas**

marbles **des billes**

martial arts **arts martiauz**

mask **un masque**

mast **un mât**

mattress **un matelas**

meadow **un champ**

measuring tape **un mètre mesureur**

medicine **un médicament**

melon **du melon**

mermaid **une sirène**

message in a bottle **un message dans une bouteille**

microwave **un four à micro-ondes**

milk **du lait**

millipede **un mille-pattes**

mirror **un miroir**

mittens **des moufles**

mixing bowl **un bol mixeur**

mobile **un mobile**

modeling clay **de la pâte à modeler**

money **de l'argent**

moneybox **une tirelire**

monkey **un singe**

mop **un balai à franges**

moth **un papillon de nuit**

mother **une mère**

motorcar **une voiture**

motor boat **un bateau à moteur**

motorbike **une motocyclette**

mountain **une montagne**

mouse **une souris**

mouth **la bouche**

muffin **un gâteau**

mug **une tasse**

mushrooms **des champignons**

music stand **un pupître**

n

nail brush **une brosse à ongles**

nails **des clous**

navy **bleu marine**

nest **un nid**

nesting box **un nichoir**

new **neuf**

newspaper **un journal**

nightie **une robe de chambre**

nine **neuf**

nineteen **dix-neuf**

Noah's ark **l'Arche de Noé**

nose **le nez**

notes **des notes**

nurse **une infirmière, un infirmier**

nuts **des fruits secs**

o

oboe **un hautbois**

octopus **une pieuvre**

off (lamp) **éteint**

old **usé**

omelette **une omelette**

on (lamp) **allumé**

one **un**

onion **un oignon**

open **ouvert**

orange (color) **orange**

orange (fruit) **une orange**

ostrich **une autruche**

outside **dehors**

oval **un ovale**

oven **une cuisinière**

owl **un hibou**

oyster **une huître**

p

packed lunch **une collation**

paddles **des pagaies**

page boy **un page**

paint **de la peinture**

paintbox **une boîte de couleurs**

paintbrush **un pinceau**

pajamas **un pyjama**

palm **la paume**

palm tree **un palmier**

panda **un panda**

pansy **une pensée**

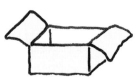

papaya **une papaye**
paper **du papier**
paper cup **un gobelet**
pantihose **des collants**
pants **un pantalon**
parachute **un parachute**
parcel **un paquet**
parrot **un perroquet**
parsnip **un panais**
party bag **une pochette-surprise**
party dress **une robe de fête**
path **un chemin**
paw **la patte**
peach **une pêche**
peacock **un paon**
pear **une poire**
pearl **une perle**
peas **des petits pois**
pebbles **des galets**
pedal car **une voiture à pédales**
pelican **un pélican**
penguin **un pingouin**
penknife **un canif**
pepper **du poivre**
personal stereo **un baladeur**
photograph **une photo**
piano **un piano**
pick-up truck **une dépanneuse**
picnic **un pique-nique**
picture **un tableau**
picture frame **un cadre**
pie **une tarte**
pig **un cochon**
pigeon **un pigeon**
piggy bank **un tirelire**
piglet **un cochonnet**
pillow **un oreiller**
pilot **un pilote**
pin board **un pense-bête**
pineapple **un ananas**

pink **rose**
pipe **une gouttière**
pirate **un pirate**
pirate flag **un drapeau de pirate**
pistol **un pistolet**
pitcher **un bol-doseur**
pizza **une pizza**
plank **une planche**
plaster **un pansement**
plaster cast **un plâtre**
plate **une assiette**
play house **casetta**
pliers **un pince**
plum **une prune**
pocket **une poche**
polar bear **un ours blanc**
pole vaulting **le saut à la perche**
pond **une mare**
poppy **un coquelicot**
porcupine **un porcépic**
portholes **des hublots**
portrait **un portrait**
poster **un poster**
potato **une pomme de terre**
potty **un ot**
praying mantis **une mante religieuse**
present **un cadeau**
prince **un prince**
princess **une princesse**
proud **être fier**
puddles **des flaques**
puffin **un macareux**
pulling **tirer**
pumpkin **une citrouille**
pupil **un élève**
puppy **un chiot**
purple **violet**
purse **un porte-monnaie**
pushing **pousser**
puzzle **un puzzle**

q

queen **une reine**
queue **une queue**

r

rabbit **un lapin**
raccoon **un raton-laveure**
racing car **une voiture de course**
radio **une radio**
radishes **des radis**
railings **une grille**
railway track **un rail de chemin de fer**
rain **la pluie**
rainbow **l'arc-en-ciel**
rake **un râteau**
raspberry **une framboise**
rattle **un hochet**
reading **lire**
recorder **un pipeau**
rectangle **un rectangle**
red **rouge**
red pepper **un poivron rouge**
refrigerator **un réfrigerateur**
refuse truck **un camion à ordures**
remote control **une télécommande**
removal van **un camion de déménagement**
rhinoceros **un rhincéros**
rhubarb **de la rhubarbe**
ribbon **un ruban**
rice **du riz**
riding (a tricycle) **faire du tricycle**
river **une rivière**
road **une route**
robot **un robot**
rocket **une fusée**
rocking chair **un fauteuil à bascule**

rocking horse **un cheval à bascule**
rocks **des rochers**
roller skating **le patin à roulettes**
rollerskates **des patins à roulettes**
rolling pin **un rouleau à pâtisserie**
roof **un toît**
roof tile **une tuile**
rope **une corde**
rose **une rose**
rowing **l'aviron**
rowing boat **une barque**
rubber ring **une bouée**
rucksack **un sac à dos**
rug **un tapis**
rugby **le rugby**
ruler **une règle**
running **courir**
runway **une piste d'atterissage**

s

sack race **la course en sac**
sad **être triste**
safety helmet **un casque**
salad **de la salade**
salt **du sel**
sand **du sable**
sandcastle **un château de sable**
sandpaper **du papier de verre**
sandpit **un bac à sable**
sandwiches **des sandwiches**
saucepan **une casserole**
saucer **une soucoupe**
sauces **des sauces**
sausages **de la charcuterie**
saw **une scie**
saxophone **un**

saxophone

scarecrow **un épouvantail**

scarf **une écharpe**

school **une école**

schoolbag **un cartable**

scissors **des ciseaux**

scooter **une trottinette**

screwdriver **un tournevis**

screws **des vis**

sea **la mer**

sea shell **un coquillage**

seahorse **un hippocampe**

seaweed **une algue**

second **second**

security light **un projecteur**

seeds **des graines**

serviette **une serviette**

seesaw **une bascule**

seven **sept**

seventeen **dix-sept**

sewing machine **une machine à coudre**

shampoo **du shampooing**

shark **un requin**

shawl **un châle**

shears **des cisailles**

shed **une cabane**

sheep **un mouton**

sheet **un drap**

sheet music **une partition**

shelf **une étagère**

shield **un bouclier**

shirt **une chemise**

shoe store **un magasin chaussures**

shoes **des chaussures**

shopper **un client**

shopping bag **un sac à provisions**

shopping cart **un caddie**

short **petit**

shorts **un short**

shoulder **l'épaule**

shower **une douche**

shower drape **un rideau de douche**

shut **fermé**

shy **être timide**

sidewalk **un trottoir**

sign **un panneau**

singing **chanter**

sink **un évier**

sister **une sœur**

sitting **être assis**

six **six**

sixteen **seize**

skateboard **une planche à roulettes**

skates **des patins**

skipping **sauter à la corde**

skipping rope **une corde à sauter**

skirt **une jupe**

skis **des skis**

skittles **des quilles**

skylight **une lucarne**

sledge **une luge**

sleeping **dormir**

sleeping bag **un sac de couchage**

sleepsuit **une grenouillère**

slice of cake **une part de gâteau**

slide **un toboggan**

sling **une écharpe**

slippers **des pantoufles**

slow **lent**

slug **une limace**

snail **un escargot**

snake **un serpent**

sneakers **des chaussures de sport**

snow **la neige**

snowflake **un flocon**

snowman **un bonhomme de neige**

soap **un savon**

soccer **le football**

socks **des chaussettes**

soda **une boisson gazeuse**

sofa **un canapé**

soil **de la terre**

soldiers **des soldats**

soother **une tétine**

sorry **être désolé**

soup **de la soupe**

spade **une pelle**

spaghetti **des spaghettis**

spanner **un clé**

spider **une araignée**

spider's web **une toile d'araignée**

sponge **une éponge**

spoon **une cuillère**

spots **des pois**

spring **le printemps**

square **un carré**

squirrel **un écureil**

stacking cups **des cônes**

standard lamp **un lampadaire**

standing **être debout**

star **une étoile**

starfish **une étoile de mer**

steamroller **un rouleau-compresseur**

stethoscope **un stéthoscope**

stewardess **une hôtesse**

stool **un tabouret**

storage jar **un bocal**

store assistant **un vendeur**

stork **une cigogne**

strawberry **une fraise**

streamers **des cotillons**

street light **un lampadaire**

street sign **un panneau**

stripes **des rayons**

submarine **un sous-marin**

sugar **du sucre**

suitcase **une valise**

summer **l'été**

sun **le soleil**

sun hat **un chapeau de paille**

sun screen **de la lotion solaire**

sunflower **un tournesol**

sunglasses **des lunettes**

sunshade **un parasol**

swallow **une hirondelle**

swan **un cygne**

sweater **un pullover**

sweet potato **une patate douce**

sweet store **une confiserie**

sweetcorn **un épi de maïs**

swimmer **un nageur**

swimming **la natation**

swimming trunks **un caleçon de bain**

swimsuit **un maillot de bain**

swing **une balançoire**

sword **une épée**

syringe **une seringue**

†

table **une table**

tablecloth **une nappe**

tablemat **un set de table**

tall **grande**

tambourine **un tambourin**

tandem **un tandem**

tangerine **un clémentine**

tanker **un camion-citerne**

tarantula **une tarantule**

tea set **une dinette**

teacher (female) **une maîtresse**

team **une équipe**

teaspoon **une petite cuillère**

teething ring **un anneau de dentition**

telephone **téléphone**

television **une télévision**

temperature chart **une courbe de température**

ten **dix**

tennis **le tennis**

tent **une tente**

thermometer **un thermomètre**

thermos flask **une bouteille thermos**

thin **mince**

third **troisième**

thirteen **treize**

thoughtful **ètre pensif**

three **trois**

three-legged race **la course à deux**

thumb **le pouce**

tickets **des billets**

tie **une cravate**

tiger **un tigre**

till **une caisse-enregistreuse**

till receipt **un ticket de caisse**

timpani **des timbales**

tissue paper **du papier toilette**

tissues **des lingettes**

toadstool **un champignon**

toaster **un grille-pain**

toe **l'orteil**

toilet **des toilettes**

tomato **un tomate**

tool box **une boîte à outils**

toothbrush **une brosse à dents**

toothpaste (tube of) **un tube de dentifrice**

top (toy) **une toupie**

top (position) **au sommet**

top hat **un chapeau claque**

tornado **une tornade**

tortoise **une tortue**

toucan **un toucan**

tractor **un tracteur**

trailer **une caravane**

trainer cup **une timbale**

trampolining **(faire du) trampoline**

trapdoor **une trappe**

trashcan **une poubelle**

tray **un plateau**

treasure **un trésor**

tree **un arbre**

trellis **une treille**

triangle **un triangle**

tricycle **un tricycle**

trolley **un chariot**

trombone **un trombone**

trophy **une coupe**

trowel **une truelle**

truck **un camion**

trumpet **une trompette**

trunk **un tronc**

T-shirt **un tee-shirt**

tummy **le ventre**

turkey **une dinde**

turnip **un navet**

turtle **une tortue marine**

twelve **douze**

twenty **vingt**

twins **des jumeaux**

two **deux**

U

uncle **un oncle**

underwear **une culotte**

up **en haut**

V

vacuum cleaner **un aspirateur**

vase **un vase**

vegetables **des légumes**

vest **un débardeur**

video **un magnétoscope**

village **un village**

vintage car **une voiture de collection**

violin **un violon**

visitor **un visiteur**

vulture **un vautour**

W

waistcoat **un gilet**

walker **un randonneur**

walking **marcher**

walking frame **un déambulateur**

walking stick **une cane**

wall tiles **des carreaux**

wallpaper **du papier peint**

wand **une baguette magique**

washbasin **un lavabo**

washcloth **une serviette**

washing **se laver**

wasp **un guèpe**

wastepaper basket **une corbeille**

watch **une montre**

water **de l'eau**

water pitcher **une carafe d'eau**

waterfall **une cascade**

watering can **un arrosoir**

water-skiing **du ski nautique**

waves **des vagues**

waving **saluer**

weightlifting **(soulever des) haltères**

wetsuit **une combinaison**

whale **une baleine**

wheelbarrow **une brouette**

wheelchair **un fauteuil roulant**

wheels **des roues**

white **blanc**

wind **le vent**

window **une fenêtre**

window box **une jardinière**

windsock **une manche à air**

wing **une aile**

winter **l'hiver**

wire basket **un panier**

wishing well **un puits magique**

wolf **un loup**

wooden spoon **un cuillère en bois**

woolly hat **un bonnet**

workbench **un établi**

worktop **un plan de travail**

worm **un ver**

wrapping paper **du papier cadeau**

wrist **le poignet**

writing **écrire**

X

xylophone **une xylophone**

Y

yacht **un voilier**

yellow **jaune**

yogurt **un yaourt**

yo-yo **un yoyo**

Z

zebra **zèbre**

zigzags **des zigzags**

zucchini **une courgette**